PAT

Written by Christine Jenkins
Illustrated by Mark Draisey

Patch was Gretchen's dog.
He had a brown patch on his nose.
Gretchen said it looked like one of Patch's doggy chews.

They were called 'Doggy Fudge Chews' because they looked like fudge. Patch loved them.

Patch liked to fetch sticks and play catch, but best of all he loved just to run about.

He was very quick.
If Gretchen could not catch him, she would go to the kitchen of her thatched house and call, "Fudge!"

Patch would run into the kitchen.
Crash!

Gretchen often took Patch to the school football pitch. One day Patch charged off over the pitch.

Patch ran into a muddy ditch.

"Oh no!" cried Gretchen.

She could not even see his patch.

When they got back, the mud had dried. It made Patch itchy. He scratched and scratched, but the mud was stuck.

It was time for a dip!

Gretchen switched on the taps.

"Into the water, Patch," she said.

But Patch ran off.
Gretchen stretched out her arms to catch him, but he ran into the kitchen.

Gretchen told Patch, "If you go in the water, you can get rid of the mud *and* your itch!"

She managed to get Patch wet,
but he did not like it.
And he charged off again.

This time Gretchen could not catch him, so she hatched a plan. She fetched a Doggy Fudge Chew.

Patch's nose twitched. Gretchen held the fudge chew and led Patch into the bath. Off came the mud!

Now Patch had a patch again, but he did not have an itch! Off he ran. **Oh no!**